Start with SCIENCE

I0893101

Weather

BY
CHARIS MATHER

KidHaven
PUBLISHING

Published in 2024 by
KidHaven Publishing, an Imprint of Greenhaven Publishing, LLC
2544 Clinton St., Buffalo, NY 14224

Written by: Charis Mather
Edited by: William Anthony
Designed by: Drue Rintoul

Photo Credits: Cover – Davidovici, ajt, CRStocker, Oleh Svetiukha, kelttt, Topdesigners, Zyn Chakrapong. 4–5 – narikan, Budimir Jevtic. 6–7 – andreiuc88, Vladimirkarp, Suwin. 8–9 – Sunny studio, Sergio Sergo. 10–11 – teh_z1b, recebin, CE Photography, kajeab_pongsiri. 12–13 – Riccardo Mayer, Vadym Zaitsev. 14–15 – AlexLinck, Afanasiev Andrii, serato. 16–17 – alexkich, Mariia Tagirova, Dan Tautan. 18–19 – Shandarov Arkadii, EndeavorMoorePhotography. 20–21 – Quirky Badger, Andrey Burmakin. 22–23 – aleksissay. All images are courtesy of Shutterstock.com, unless otherwise specified. With thanks to Getty Images, Thinkstock Photo and iStockphoto.

Cataloging-in-Publication Data

Names: Mather, Charis
Title: Weather / Charis Mather.
Description: New York : KidHaven Publishing, 2024. | Series: Start with science | Includes glossary and index.
Identifiers: ISBN 9781534544925 (pbk) | ISBN 9781534544932 (library bound) | ISBN 9781534544949 (ebook)
Subjects: LCSH: Weather-- Juvenile literature
Classification: LCC QC981.3 M38 2024 | DDC 551.6 --dc23

Manufactured in the United States of America

CPSIA compliance information: Batch #CSKH24: For further information contact Greenhaven Publishing LLC at 1-844-317-7404.

Please visit our website, www.greenhavenpublishing.com.
For a free color catalog of all our high-quality books, call toll free 1-844-317-7404 or fax 1-844-317-7405.

Find us on

Contents

Words that look like **this** can be found in the glossary on page 24.

Think LIKE A Scientist

Scientists are people who learn about the world and how it changes. They usually have certain topics that they find out about. Some scientists know a lot about the weather.

When scientists want to find out something they do not know, they can use different tools to help them. Scientists make notes about what they learn and share them with others.

These scientists are using a tool to learn about the rain.

Weather

Weather is what is happening in the sky and in the air around us. The weather can change every day. Rain, snow, and sunshine are all types of weather.

Scientists use tools to measure changes in the weather. They can look at weather over large or small areas. Scientists need different tools to learn about different types of weather.

Sunshine

When clouds are not in the way of the sun's light, the weather is sunny. The sky is often a clear blue color. Sunshine can often feel warm.

The light and heat that come from the sun are very important to living things. The sun's heat can be measured with a tool called a thermometer. Sunlight can also help to dry up wet areas.

Thermometers have numbers that tell scientists how hot or cold something is.

Clouds

When sunlight dries up water, it goes into the air. The water in the air comes together into tiny **droplets**. The droplets make up clouds that look like white or gray shapes.

Clouds sometimes look soft and fluffy.

Clouds come in all sorts of different shapes. Sometimes they are long and thin. Sometimes they are grouped up and thick. Scientists have names for the different types of clouds.

Rain

Water in the clouds sometimes falls out of the sky. This is called rain. Rain happens when the water droplets in the clouds get so large and heavy that they cannot stay in the sky.

Scientists use a tool called a rain gauge to measure how much rain has fallen. After it rains, scientists write down how much water is in the rain gauge.

Wind

Windy weather is caused by warm and cold air. When air gets warm, it moves upward into the sky. As warm air leaves a space, colder air moves in to fill it. This moving air is called wind.

Hot-air balloons trap warm air so that they move upward.

Scientists are interested in how fast the wind is and which way it is going. They use tools to measure the speed and direction of the wind.

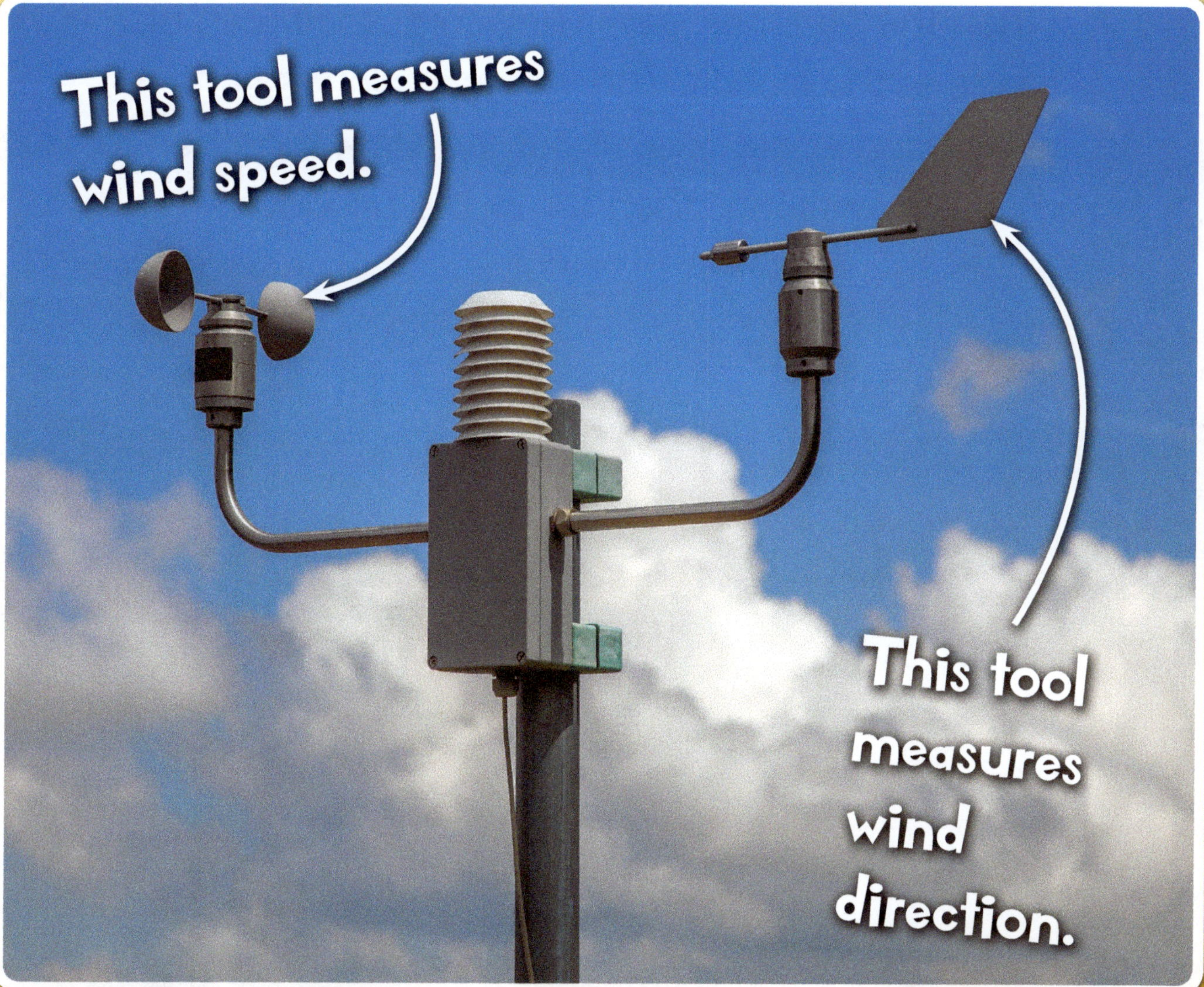

Snow AND Hail

When the weather gets very cold, snow can be made in the clouds. The water in clouds can freeze and become ice. The bits of ice stick together to make snowflakes, then fall to the ground.

The bits of ice in snowflakes make interesting patterns.

When it is windy and cold, frozen water droplets in the clouds can turn into hail. Hail is made of hailstones, which are balls of ice. Hailstones are usually smaller than a pea.

Thunderstorms

Sometimes, weather can be dangerous. Thunderstorms are a type of dangerous weather. They can have heavy winds, rain, thunder, and lightning. People have to be careful during thunderstorms.

Thunderstorms usually have dark clouds.

Lightning is a very hot, bright flash of light that happens during thunderstorms. Thunder is the loud, rumbling sound that lightning makes.

When lightning happens far away, you can see it before you hear it.

IN THE Real World

Weather can make big changes to the world. Wind can push down trees. Too much sunny weather without rain can lead to fires. Too much rain can cause flooding.

Scientists help people get ready for bad weather. By understanding how the weather works, scientists can guess when the weather will cause problems. This is called weather **forecasting**.

Be A Scientist

Make your own paper windmill to test how fast the wind is blowing. Get a grown-up to help.

STEP 1: Cut the corners of a square piece of paper toward the middle. Leave the middle uncut.

STEP 2: Bend one corner of each section into the middle. Glue the same corner of every section.

STEP 3: Carefully put a pin through the middle of the paper. Add a straw to hold your new windmill.

Glossary

DIRECTION the way that someone or something is moving or pointing

DROPLET a very small drop of something, such as water

FLOODING when a normally dry area is covered by water

FORECASTING making a guess based on information from tools and things that can be seen

FREEZE to harden into ice because of cold temperatures

MEASURE to use a tool to find out or record the amount of something

RUMBLING a deep sound that continues for a little while

SPEED how fast or slow something or someone is

TOOL a piece of equipment that is used for a specific reason

Index